THE 3-MINUTE

Unicorn

LEADERSHIP JOURNAL

FOR KIDS

____

✏ THIS AWESOME JOURNAL BELONGS TO:

Blank Classic

The 3-Minute Unicorn
        Leadership Journal for Kids
116 numbered pages - 120 total pages
A5 (5.83 x 8.27)

Design © 2021 Blank Classic

Blank Classic

Mailing address:
Blank Classic
PO BOX 4608
Main Station Terminal
349 West Georgia Street
Vancouver, BC
Canada, V6B 4A1

Cover design by: Lauren Dick
Interior design by: Lauren Dick

ISBN: 978-1-77476-178-6

FIRST EDITION / FIRST PRINTING

I CAN...

SHOW KINDNESS

SET GOALS

HELP PEOPLE

INSPIRE PEOPLE

LEARN FROM OTHERS

BELIEVE IN MYSELF

SET A GOOD EXAMPLE

ADMIT MISTAKES

EMBRACE DIFFERENCES

BE A GOOD LISTENER

BECAUSE I AM A **LEADER**

SIGNED,

____

DATE: S M T W TH F S   __ / __ / __

OVERALL TODAY WAS: ☆ ☆ ☆ ☆ ☆

😄 TODAY'S TRIUMPHS

____
____
____
____
____
____
____
____
____
____

😋 TODAY'S CHALLENGES

____
____
____
____
____
____
____
____
____
____

💡 WHAT I LEARNED FROM TODAY:

____

🏆 MY TOP GOAL FOR TOMORROW:

____

DRAW ABOUT IT

DATE: S M T W TH F S   __ / __ / __

🎲 OVERALL TODAY WAS: ☆ ☆ ☆ ☆ ☆

😄 TODAY'S TRIUMPHS

____
____
____
____
____
____
____
____
____

🤔 TODAY'S CHALLENGES

____
____
____
____
____
____
____
____
____

💡 WHAT I LEARNED FROM TODAY:

____

🏆 MY TOP GOAL FOR TOMORROW:

____

DRAW ABOUT IT

DATE: S M T W TH F S __ / __ / __

OVERALL TODAY WAS: ☆ ☆ ☆ ☆ ☆

😄 TODAY'S TRIUMPHS

____
____
____
____
____
____
____
____
____

🤭 TODAY'S CHALLENGES

____
____
____
____
____
____
____
____
____

💡 WHAT I LEARNED FROM TODAY:

____

🏆 MY TOP GOAL FOR TOMORROW:

____

DRAW ABOUT IT

DATE: S M T W TH F S   __ / __ /__

OVERALL TODAY WAS: ☆ ☆ ☆ ☆ ☆

😄 TODAY'S TRIUMPHS

😋 TODAY'S CHALLENGES

💡 WHAT I LEARNED FROM TODAY:

🏆 MY TOP GOAL FOR TOMORROW:

DRAW ABOUT IT

DATE: S M T W TH F S ___ / ___ / ___

🏆 OVERALL TODAY WAS: ☆ ☆ ☆ ☆ ☆

😄 TODAY'S TRIUMPHS

🤔 TODAY'S CHALLENGES

💡 WHAT I LEARNED FROM TODAY:

🏆 MY TOP GOAL FOR TOMORROW:

DRAW ABOUT IT

DATE: S M T W TH F S   __ / __ /__

📊 OVERALL TODAY WAS: ☆ ☆ ☆ ☆ ☆

😄 TODAY'S TRIUMPHS

____
____
____
____
____
____
____
____

🤭 TODAY'S CHALLENGES

____
____
____
____
____
____
____
____

💡 WHAT I LEARNED FROM TODAY:

____

🏆 MY TOP GOAL FOR TOMORROW:

____

DRAW ABOUT IT

DATE: S M T W TH F S   __ / __ / __

⊞ OVERALL TODAY WAS: ☆ ☆ ☆ ☆ ☆

😊 TODAY'S TRIUMPHS

🤔 TODAY'S CHALLENGES

💡 WHAT I LEARNED FROM TODAY:

🏆 MY TOP GOAL FOR TOMORROW:

DRAW ABOUT IT

DATE: S M T W TH F S __ / __ / __

🧱 OVERALL TODAY WAS: ☆ ☆ ☆ ☆ ☆

😄 TODAY'S TRIUMPHS

____
____
____
____
____
____
____
____

🤔 TODAY'S CHALLENGES

____
____
____
____
____
____
____
____

💡 WHAT I LEARNED FROM TODAY:

____

🏆 MY TOP GOAL FOR TOMORROW:

____

DRAW ABOUT IT

DATE: S M T W TH F S __ / __ / __

⊞ OVERALL TODAY WAS: ☆ ☆ ☆ ☆ ☆

😀 TODAY'S TRIUMPHS

😋 TODAY'S CHALLENGES

💡 WHAT I LEARNED FROM TODAY:

🏆 MY TOP GOAL FOR TOMORROW:

DRAW ABOUT IT

DATE: S M T W TH F S ___ / ___ / ___

OVERALL TODAY WAS: ☆ ☆ ☆ ☆ ☆

😄 TODAY'S TRIUMPHS

🤔 TODAY'S CHALLENGES

💡 WHAT I LEARNED FROM TODAY:

🏆 MY TOP GOAL FOR TOMORROW:

DRAW ABOUT IT

DATE: S M T W TH F S __ / __ / __

😄 TODAY'S TRIUMPHS

____
____
____
____
____
____
____
____

🤭 TODAY'S CHALLENGES

____
____
____
____
____
____
____
____

💡 WHAT I LEARNED FROM TODAY:

____

🏆 MY TOP GOAL FOR TOMORROW:

____

DRAW ABOUT IT

DATE: S M T W TH F S __/__/__

😀 TODAY'S TRIUMPHS

____
____
____
____
____
____
____

😛 TODAY'S CHALLENGES

____
____
____
____
____
____
____

💡 WHAT I LEARNED FROM TODAY:

____

🏆 MY TOP GOAL FOR TOMORROW:

____

DRAW ABOUT IT

DATE: S M T W TH F S __ / __ / __

🏆 OVERALL TODAY WAS: ☆ ☆ ☆ ☆ ☆

😄 TODAY'S TRIUMPHS

____
____
____
____
____
____
____
____

🤔 TODAY'S CHALLENGES

____
____
____
____
____
____
____
____

💡 WHAT I LEARNED FROM TODAY:

____

🏆 MY TOP GOAL FOR TOMORROW:

____

DATE: S M T W TH F S   __ / __ /__

🧱 OVERALL TODAY WAS: ☆ ☆ ☆ ☆ ☆

😄 TODAY'S TRIUMPHS

____

____

____

____

____

____

____

____

____

____

🤔 TODAY'S CHALLENGES

____

____

____

____

____

____

____

____

____

____

💡 WHAT I LEARNED FROM TODAY:

____

🏆 MY TOP GOAL FOR TOMORROW:

____

DRAW ABOUT IT

DATE: S M T W TH F S __ / __ / __

OVERALL TODAY WAS: ☆ ☆ ☆ ☆ ☆

😄 TODAY'S TRIUMPHS

🤭 TODAY'S CHALLENGES

💡 WHAT I LEARNED FROM TODAY:

🏆 MY TOP GOAL FOR TOMORROW:

DRAW ABOUT IT

DATE: S M T W TH F S   __ / __ /__

🏆 OVERALL TODAY WAS: ☆ ☆ ☆ ☆ ☆

😄 TODAY'S TRIUMPHS

____
____
____
____
____
____
____
____

🤭 TODAY'S CHALLENGES

____
____
____
____
____
____
____
____

💡 WHAT I LEARNED FROM TODAY:

____

🏆 MY TOP GOAL FOR TOMORROW:

____

DRAW ABOUT IT

DATE: S M T W TH F S __ / __ / __

OVERALL TODAY WAS: ☆ ☆ ☆ ☆ ☆

😄 TODAY'S TRIUMPHS

____
____
____
____
____
____
____
____

🤔 TODAY'S CHALLENGES

____
____
____
____
____
____
____
____

💡 WHAT I LEARNED FROM TODAY:

____

🏆 MY TOP GOAL FOR TOMORROW:

____

DRAW ABOUT IT

DATE: S M T W TH F S ___ / ___ / ___

OVERALL TODAY WAS: ☆ ☆ ☆ ☆ ☆

😄 TODAY'S TRIUMPHS

🤔 TODAY'S CHALLENGES

💡 WHAT I LEARNED FROM TODAY:

🏆 MY TOP GOAL FOR TOMORROW:

DRAW ABOUT IT

DATE: S M T W TH F S __ / __ / __

OVERALL TODAY WAS: ☆ ☆ ☆ ☆ ☆

😄 TODAY'S TRIUMPHS

🤔 TODAY'S CHALLENGES

💡 WHAT I LEARNED FROM TODAY:

🏆 MY TOP GOAL FOR TOMORROW:

DRAW ABOUT IT

DATE: S M T W TH F S __ / __ / __

🏆 OVERALL TODAY WAS: ☆ ☆ ☆ ☆ ☆

😄 TODAY'S TRIUMPHS

🤔 TODAY'S CHALLENGES

💡 WHAT I LEARNED FROM TODAY:

🏆 MY TOP GOAL FOR TOMORROW:

DRAW ABOUT IT

DATE: S M T W TH F S __ / __ / __

😄 OVERALL TODAY WAS: ☆ ☆ ☆ ☆ ☆

😊 TODAY'S TRIUMPHS

😛 TODAY'S CHALLENGES

💡 WHAT I LEARNED FROM TODAY:

🏆 MY TOP GOAL FOR TOMORROW:

DRAW ABOUT IT

DATE: S M T W TH F S __ / __ / __

OVERALL TODAY WAS: ☆ ☆ ☆ ☆ ☆

😄 TODAY'S TRIUMPHS

😋 TODAY'S CHALLENGES

💡 WHAT I LEARNED FROM TODAY:

🏆 MY TOP GOAL FOR TOMORROW:

DRAW ABOUT IT

DATE: S M T W TH F S   __ / __ / __

OVERALL TODAY WAS: ☆ ☆ ☆ ☆ ☆

😊 TODAY'S TRIUMPHS

____
____
____
____
____
____
____
____
____

🤔 TODAY'S CHALLENGES

____
____
____
____
____
____
____
____
____

💡 WHAT I LEARNED FROM TODAY:

____

🏆 MY TOP GOAL FOR TOMORROW:

____

DRAW ABOUT IT

DATE: S M T W TH F S   __ / __ /__

OVERALL TODAY WAS: ☆ ☆ ☆ ☆ ☆

😄 TODAY'S TRIUMPHS

____
____
____
____
____
____
____
____

🤔 TODAY'S CHALLENGES

____
____
____
____
____
____
____
____

💡 WHAT I LEARNED FROM TODAY:

____

🏆 MY TOP GOAL FOR TOMORROW:

____

DRAW ABOUT IT

DATE: S   M   T   W   TH   F   S   __ / __ /__

OVERALL TODAY WAS: ☆ ☆ ☆ ☆ ☆

😄 TODAY'S TRIUMPHS

🤔 TODAY'S CHALLENGES

💡 WHAT I LEARNED FROM TODAY:

🏆 MY TOP GOAL FOR TOMORROW:

DRAW ABOUT IT

DATE: S M T W TH F S __ / __ /__

OVERALL TODAY WAS: ☆ ☆ ☆ ☆ ☆

😄 TODAY'S TRIUMPHS

____

____

____

____

____

____

____

____

____

____

🤔 TODAY'S CHALLENGES

____

____

____

____

____

____

____

____

____

____

💡 WHAT I LEARNED FROM TODAY:

____

🏆 MY TOP GOAL FOR TOMORROW:

____

DRAW ABOUT IT

DATE: S   M   T   W   TH   F   S   __ / __ / __

OVERALL TODAY WAS: ☆ ☆ ☆ ☆ ☆

😄 TODAY'S TRIUMPHS

____
____
____
____
____
____
____
____

🤔 TODAY'S CHALLENGES

____
____
____
____
____
____
____
____

💡 WHAT I LEARNED FROM TODAY:

____

🏆 MY TOP GOAL FOR TOMORROW:

____

DRAW ABOUT IT

DATE: S M T W TH F S __ / __ / __

😄 TODAY'S TRIUMPHS

🤔 TODAY'S CHALLENGES

____
____
____
____
____
____
____
____

💡 WHAT I LEARNED FROM TODAY:

____

🏆 MY TOP GOAL FOR TOMORROW:

____

DRAW ABOUT IT

DATE: S M T W TH F S __ / __ /__

OVERALL TODAY WAS: ☆ ☆ ☆ ☆ ☆

😄 TODAY'S TRIUMPHS

🤭 TODAY'S CHALLENGES

💡 WHAT I LEARNED FROM TODAY:

🏆 MY TOP GOAL FOR TOMORROW:

DRAW ABOUT IT

DATE: S M T W TH F S   __ / __ / __

🏆 OVERALL TODAY WAS: ☆ ☆ ☆ ☆ ☆

😊 TODAY'S TRIUMPHS

____

____

____

____

____

____

____

____

😋 TODAY'S CHALLENGES

____

____

____

____

____

____

____

____

💡 WHAT I LEARNED FROM TODAY:

____

🏆 MY TOP GOAL FOR TOMORROW:

____

DRAW ABOUT IT

OVERALL TODAY WAS: ☆ ☆ ☆ ☆ ☆

😄 TODAY'S TRIUMPHS

____
____
____
____
____
____
____
____
____

🤔 TODAY'S CHALLENGES

____
____
____
____
____
____
____
____
____

💡 WHAT I LEARNED FROM TODAY:

____

🏆 MY TOP GOAL FOR TOMORROW:

____

DRAW ABOUT IT

DATE: S M T W TH F S __ / __ /__

📊 OVERALL TODAY WAS: ☆ ☆ ☆ ☆ ☆

😃 TODAY'S TRIUMPHS

🤔 TODAY'S CHALLENGES

💡 WHAT I LEARNED FROM TODAY:

🏆 MY TOP GOAL FOR TOMORROW:

DRAW ABOUT IT

DATE: S   M   T   W   TH   F   S   __ / __ / __

🏆 **OVERALL TODAY WAS:**   ☆ ☆ ☆ ☆ ☆

😄 **TODAY'S TRIUMPHS**

____
____
____
____
____
____
____
____

🤔 **TODAY'S CHALLENGES**

____
____
____
____
____
____
____
____

💡 **WHAT I LEARNED FROM TODAY:**

____

🏆 **MY TOP GOAL FOR TOMORROW:**

____

DATE: S M T W TH F S   __ / __ /__

OVERALL TODAY WAS: ☆ ☆ ☆ ☆ ☆

😄 TODAY'S TRIUMPHS

🤭 TODAY'S CHALLENGES

💡 WHAT I LEARNED FROM TODAY:

🏆 MY TOP GOAL FOR TOMORROW:

DRAW ABOUT IT

DATE: S M T W TH F S __ / __ /__

OVERALL TODAY WAS: ☆ ☆ ☆ ☆ ☆

😊 TODAY'S TRIUMPHS

🤭 TODAY'S CHALLENGES

💡 WHAT I LEARNED FROM TODAY:

🏆 MY TOP GOAL FOR TOMORROW:

DRAW ABOUT IT

DATE: S M T W TH F S __ / __ / __

🔢 OVERALL TODAY WAS: ☆ ☆ ☆ ☆ ☆

😄 TODAY'S TRIUMPHS

____

____

____

____

____

____

____

____

🤔 TODAY'S CHALLENGES

____

____

____

____

____

____

____

____

💡 WHAT I LEARNED FROM TODAY:

____

🏆 MY TOP GOAL FOR TOMORROW:

____

DRAW ABOUT IT

DATE: S M T W TH F S   __ / __ /__

OVERALL TODAY WAS: ☆ ☆ ☆ ☆ ☆

😄 TODAY'S TRIUMPHS

🤭 TODAY'S CHALLENGES

💡 WHAT I LEARNED FROM TODAY:

🏆 MY TOP GOAL FOR TOMORROW:

DRAW ABOUT IT

DATE: S M T W TH F S __ / __ / __

OVERALL TODAY WAS: ☆ ☆ ☆ ☆ ☆

😄 TODAY'S TRIUMPHS

____
____
____
____
____
____
____
____
____

🤔 TODAY'S CHALLENGES

____
____
____
____
____
____
____
____
____

💡 WHAT I LEARNED FROM TODAY:

____

🏆 MY TOP GOAL FOR TOMORROW:

____

DRAW ABOUT IT

DATE: S M T W TH F S __ / __ / __

Overall Today Was: ☆ ☆ ☆ ☆ ☆

😄 TODAY'S TRIUMPHS

____
____
____
____
____
____
____
____

🤭 TODAY'S CHALLENGES

____
____
____
____
____
____
____
____

💡 WHAT I LEARNED FROM TODAY:

____

🏆 MY TOP GOAL FOR TOMORROW:

____

DRAW ABOUT IT

DATE: S M T W TH F S   __ / __ / __

🏆 OVERALL TODAY WAS: ☆ ☆ ☆ ☆ ☆

😄 TODAY'S TRIUMPHS

____
____
____
____
____
____
____
____
____

🤭 TODAY'S CHALLENGES

____
____
____
____
____
____
____
____
____

💡 WHAT I LEARNED FROM TODAY:

____

🏆 MY TOP GOAL FOR TOMORROW:

____

DRAW ABOUT IT

DATE: S M T W TH F S   __ / __ / __

📊 OVERALL TODAY WAS: ☆ ☆ ☆ ☆ ☆

😄 TODAY'S TRIUMPHS

____
____
____
____
____
____
____
____

🤔 TODAY'S CHALLENGES

____
____
____
____
____
____
____
____

💡 WHAT I LEARNED FROM TODAY:

____

🏆 MY TOP GOAL FOR TOMORROW:

____

DRAW ABOUT IT

DATE: S M T W TH F S __ / __ / __

OVERALL TODAY WAS: ☆ ☆ ☆ ☆ ☆

😊 TODAY'S TRIUMPHS

🤔 TODAY'S CHALLENGES

💡 WHAT I LEARNED FROM TODAY:

🏆 MY TOP GOAL FOR TOMORROW:

DRAW ABOUT IT

DATE: S   M   T   W   TH   F   S   __ / __ / __

🧊 OVERALL TODAY WAS: ☆ ☆ ☆ ☆ ☆

😊 TODAY'S TRIUMPHS

____
____
____
____
____
____
____
____

😋 TODAY'S CHALLENGES

____
____
____
____
____
____
____
____

💡 WHAT I LEARNED FROM TODAY:

____

🏆 MY TOP GOAL FOR TOMORROW:

____

DRAW ABOUT IT

DATE: S M T W TH F S ___ / ___ / ___

🧊 OVERALL TODAY WAS: ☆ ☆ ☆ ☆ ☆

😄 TODAY'S TRIUMPHS

😛 TODAY'S CHALLENGES

💡 WHAT I LEARNED FROM TODAY:

🏆 MY TOP GOAL FOR TOMORROW:

DRAW ABOUT IT

DATE: S M T W TH F S   __ / __ /__

OVERALL TODAY WAS: ☆ ☆ ☆ ☆ ☆

😄 TODAY'S TRIUMPHS

____
____
____
____
____
____
____
____

🤭 TODAY'S CHALLENGES

____
____
____
____
____
____
____
____

💡 WHAT I LEARNED FROM TODAY:

____

🏆 MY TOP GOAL FOR TOMORROW:

____

DRAW ABOUT IT

DATE: S M T W TH F S __ / __ /__

🏆 OVERALL TODAY WAS: ☆ ☆ ☆ ☆ ☆

😄 TODAY'S TRIUMPHS

🤔 TODAY'S CHALLENGES

💡 WHAT I LEARNED FROM TODAY:

🏆 MY TOP GOAL FOR TOMORROW:

DRAW ABOUT IT

OVERALL TODAY WAS: ☆ ☆ ☆ ☆ ☆

TODAY'S TRIUMPHS

____
____
____
____
____
____
____
____

TODAY'S CHALLENGES

____
____
____
____
____
____
____
____

WHAT I LEARNED FROM TODAY:

____

MY TOP GOAL FOR TOMORROW:

____

DRAW ABOUT IT

DATE: S M T W TH F S __ / __ / __

OVERALL TODAY WAS: ☆ ☆ ☆ ☆ ☆

😊 TODAY'S TRIUMPHS

🤔 TODAY'S CHALLENGES

💡 WHAT I LEARNED FROM TODAY:

🏆 MY TOP GOAL FOR TOMORROW:

DRAW ABOUT IT

DATE: S   M   T   W   TH   F   S   __ / __ / __

🏆 OVERALL TODAY WAS: ☆ ☆ ☆ ☆ ☆

😄 TODAY'S TRIUMPHS

____
____
____
____
____
____
____
____

🤔 TODAY'S CHALLENGES

____
____
____
____
____
____
____
____

💡 WHAT I LEARNED FROM TODAY:

____

🏆 MY TOP GOAL FOR TOMORROW:

____

DRAW ABOUT IT

DATE: S M T W TH F S __ / __ / __

🏆 OVERALL TODAY WAS: ☆ ☆ ☆ ☆ ☆

😋 TODAY'S TRIUMPHS

____
____
____
____
____
____
____
____

🤔 TODAY'S CHALLENGES

____
____
____
____
____
____
____
____

💡 WHAT I LEARNED FROM TODAY:

____

🏆 MY TOP GOAL FOR TOMORROW:

____

DRAW ABOUT IT

DATE: S M T W TH F S __ / __ / __

☺ TODAY'S TRIUMPHS

😛 TODAY'S CHALLENGES

💡 WHAT I LEARNED FROM TODAY:

🏆 MY TOP GOAL FOR TOMORROW:

DRAW ABOUT IT

DATE: S M T W TH F S __ / __ / __

OVERALL TODAY WAS: ☆ ☆ ☆ ☆ ☆

😄 TODAY'S TRIUMPHS

🤔 TODAY'S CHALLENGES

💡 WHAT I LEARNED FROM TODAY:

🏆 MY TOP GOAL FOR TOMORROW:

DRAW ABOUT IT

DATE: S   M   T   W   TH   F   S   __ / __ / __

OVERALL TODAY WAS: ☆ ☆ ☆ ☆ ☆

☺ TODAY'S TRIUMPHS

☺ TODAY'S CHALLENGES

WHAT I LEARNED FROM TODAY:

MY TOP GOAL FOR TOMORROW:

OVERALL TODAY WAS: ☆ ☆ ☆ ☆ ☆

😄 TODAY'S TRIUMPHS

____
____
____
____
____
____
____
____

🤭 TODAY'S CHALLENGES

____
____
____
____
____
____
____
____

💡 WHAT I LEARNED FROM TODAY:

____

🏆 MY TOP GOAL FOR TOMORROW:

____

DRAW ABOUT IT

DATE: S M T W TH F S __ / __ / __

OVERALL TODAY WAS: ☆ ☆ ☆ ☆ ☆

😊 TODAY'S TRIUMPHS

🤭 TODAY'S CHALLENGES

💡 WHAT I LEARNED FROM TODAY:

🏆 MY TOP GOAL FOR TOMORROW:

DRAW ABOUT IT

DATE: S M T W TH F S ___ / __ /__

🎲 OVERALL TODAY WAS: ☆ ☆ ☆ ☆ ☆

😋 TODAY'S TRIUMPHS

____
____
____
____
____
____
____
____
____

🤭 TODAY'S CHALLENGES

____
____
____
____
____
____
____
____
____

💡 WHAT I LEARNED FROM TODAY:

____

🏆 MY TOP GOAL FOR TOMORROW:

____

DRAW ABOUT IT

DATE: S M T W TH F S __ / __ / __

OVERALL TODAY WAS: ☆ ☆ ☆ ☆ ☆

😄 TODAY'S TRIUMPHS

😋 TODAY'S CHALLENGES

💡 WHAT I LEARNED FROM TODAY:

🏆 MY TOP GOAL FOR TOMORROW:

DRAW ABOUT IT

DATE: S M T W TH F S   __ / __ / __

😊 OVERALL TODAY WAS: ☆ ☆ ☆ ☆ ☆

😊 TODAY'S TRIUMPHS

🤭 TODAY'S CHALLENGES

💡 WHAT I LEARNED FROM TODAY:

🏆 MY TOP GOAL FOR TOMORROW:

DRAW ABOUT IT

www.ingramcontent.com/pod-product-compliance
Lightning Source LLC
Chambersburg PA
CBHW060953050726
47592CB00003B/1211